THE STONER'S COLORING BOOK

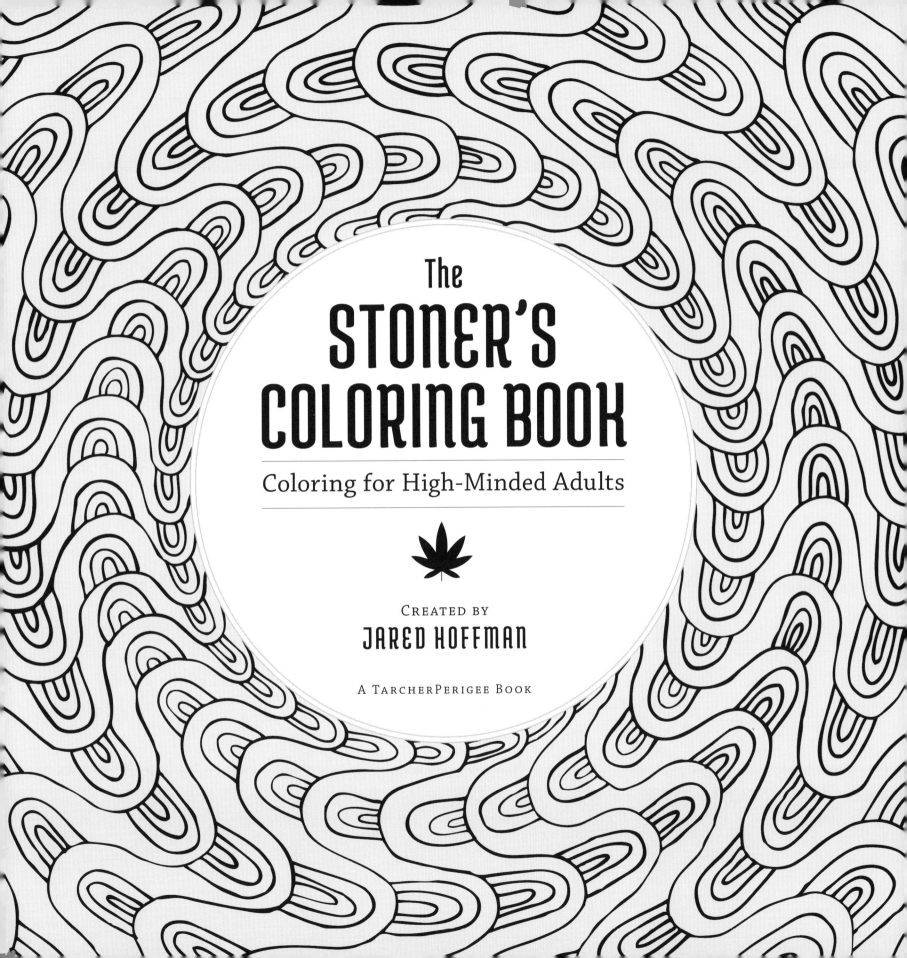

The
STONER'S
COLORING BOOK

Coloring for High-Minded Adults

CREATED BY
JARED HOFFMAN

A TarcherPerigee Book

tarcherperigee

An imprint of Penguin Random House LLC
375 Hudson Street
New York, New York 10014

Original edition published by Jared Hoffman

TarcherPerigee and the TarcherPerigee colophon are registered
trademarks of Penguin Random House LLC.

Most TarcherPerigee books are available at special quantity
discounts for bulk purchase for sales promotions, premiums,
fund-raising, and educational needs. Special books or book
excerpts also can be created to fit specific needs. For details,
write: SpecialMarkets@penguinrandomhouse.com.

ISBN 9780143130291

Printed in China
7   9   10   8

2

Emma Gelbard

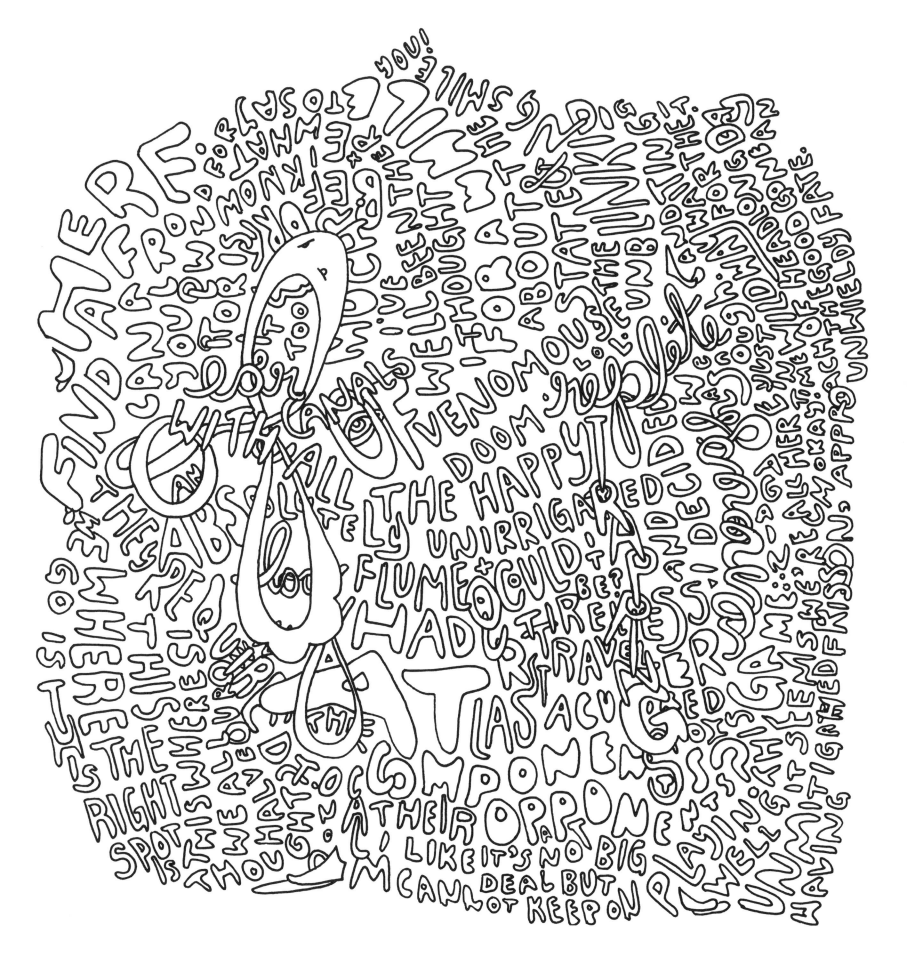

Sebastián Cola

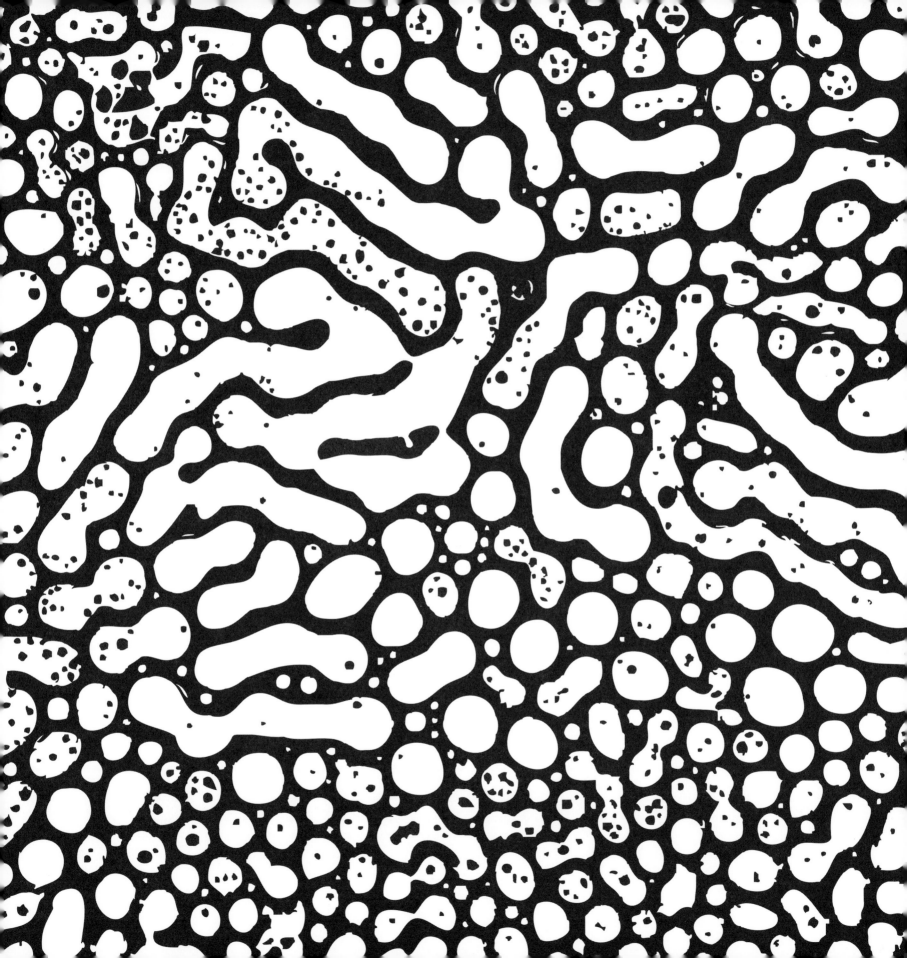

Bridget Klappert

Emma Gelbard

Audrey Ryals

Kalen Blackburn

44
Aneri Pandya

Kalen Blackburn

Bridget Klappert

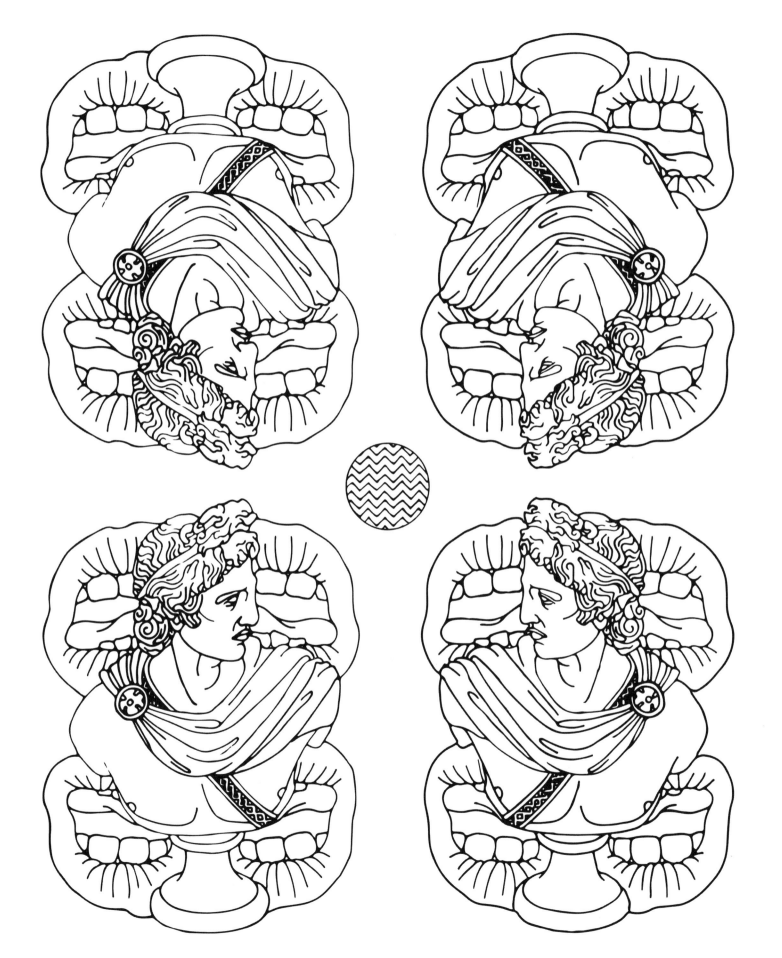

Lucia Nayoon Lee

Kalen Blackburn

Janet Koelle

Emma Gelbard

Bridget Klappert

86 (also p. 1)
Kalen Blackburn

You Are the Spark

This project was originally made possible by 370 Kickstarter backers who funded this book on nothing more than a joint and a dream. To all those who made this possible: you light my fire.

Acknowledgments: Juicy, Sara Meshael Garcia, Whittney & Alberto, a simple man who likes to color, ???, Philly Blunts Kim, dick cheney, Noah Grossman-look I don't have much time I've hidden the diamonds withi, The Big Veet, Mitch "Send It!" Burns, Postal, DJ B.ill & the Linden lunatics, No credit necessary, Tabby and Mr. Swisher the titty twister, Debbie, PalRoss and Angela, Kofi Kush, kfreeze19, B. On The Mountain, Ponie & Doobie Frueh, Lynnae Stoehr, Andrew Palmer, Sunshine Ray Aranda, Happy Birthday Zach!, The Girl Who Said She'd Have A Foursome, Carol Harrison 45 years a stoner, @eric_wallace_8 LEDN, my degenerates, Jolene Ha, The best bro ever MadBradley, L-Sunkisd, Chainsaw Communications, Carli Ebbert, SRD & ELF 4ever, Jennifer McAuley, a hip old chick who still loves to color, Island of Misfit Toys, Marcy and Cindy, Wendy and Handy, Dina, AdventuringLink, Iggy Dauchot & Aimee Welch—happy coloring!, Bradshaw-Burfords, Syd the Kyd & Emilio!, Johnny (scooterpie) Wiggs—Cannabis Connoisseur, Michelle Trudeau, I'm way too high for this shit right now, Tati ur my fav stoner—I <3 U—Chris, Fellow Stoners UNITE, When you smoke herb it reveals you to yourself—Kate & Jake, Gillian and Lauren Bee, Danni "Black Hawk" & Nikki "Wolf Rider," Susan and Ralph Paglia—with Nicole Pitcher, Kathy B, Yoshi Andersen and Melena Masson, Just Chill Ryan @rd_nice, Arwen & Ziva '15, Richard Wood and Robert his pet rabbit, Big Up to Creese's Creases & his lover Jessie T!, Timbrely Pearsley & Andy Feld, Spanj Spanj, Mitzi & Annsley, two old hippies from Syracuse, Stay lifted & gifted!!—Biscuit & Gravy, Don't credit me please, I'm just so glad you succeeded! Rah!, Chris & Katherine, Michelle Lorenz & Dan DeLaTorre, David H-Patron of the Arts (and coloring), Tina—always loved coloring!, Marki Jean, Color me, The Goodman-Bernstein Center, Betsy Woodin, clouding around w/ Janice and 109 4th FL, koala loves panda, The Viper and Little Dubious, Sara Skillz, possiBri, Rhonda Fisekci, Bonnie Erin Badass, Brown Sugar, Food makes poop, Veronica Harrington is a terrible person, Steve Branson, The Pious Piper, Betsy Jameson, Darla & Staci Singletary, Grant Melinek aka Jeremy Pancakes, always believe in your creativity—Max, James Ghilardi, Chris W <3 dabs 4ever xoxo #ATL, I don't even smoke ahahahah, witchywomin, a dope guy, Thunder and Snowy :3, Grandma, Kurt Godel, Fat Tire Massive, REB JR, Kitty Wonka, Amigos De Garcia Productions, Thank you Almighty, to Victoria, color on!, Suzy Boozy Gonzalez & Ziggy Mo, Anthony OA Russo, Leslie, Patricia Williams, Sara highly-minded Nachum, Skye Collins~stonerdragonlady, Pearl Simard Supertramp RN BSN, LadyMarilynExquisita~Baltimore, MD, Special thanks to Laidback Industries, Dina Vasquez, Jess Compton, Tammy Loves Philip, Sam Schiebold, Chad W, thanks to Ana Kenny Slye for her generous donation, Kristi Anne Beams-Living Awesomeness :), Sky Wizard Annelise, "Just color bro," I don't understand the question, thank you!, Head Stoner Artist's mom's friend AB, Alexandria "Cheech" Schaum, Alexis Stonzza, Kevin Clam, Danklord Supreme (Korty), Laische Zimm 710, Vice Yarns, Jeff and Hemi, Jacob Wang, Princess Crosspaw, Bill Hewson, Sujin Han, Robin D.R. and Mike McKenna, LDogg Cramer, Mr. Hash Bash—Adam L. Brook . . . color on!, Carino, Inspirations for Erica of Dye on the Fly, Darren Chen, Nick Philpot, A. ClarkSturm, Crystal Melody Trotter *Saturn Ascends*, A vintage stoner with an appreciation for artistic endeavors, Brian Henze, For Turtles everywere; Honu., Portia R. Thomas, Patrick Z. & Marc K. USFIV Bros 2015, Andrew Grimnes, Penn Payungcharoen + Todd Kueny Jr, Lisa Wang, MoiMoi, AfroPuff, Charlie Craig, Badass Suzanne Ashley Herrmann bitch, Mariah Bolton, M.A.A., Mendocino Group, Abbey Anders, Spencer *Ponyo* Serrano, Eddie G, Stephanie J Plaza, Wake N Bake! Corey Gault+Lindsay Miller, Jack O, Things are more like they are now than they have ever been before! <3 SK, End the failed drug war now . . . Legalize!, DLH, Xotic Delivery, these Damn Hippies and their Devil's Lettuce, and Bailey.

Thanks to all the artists who participated in this collaborative project! Thank you to the TarcherPerigee team for their hard work spreading the light of this book around the world. To Alyssa, thank you for guiding and advising me. Thank you to Grandma and Poppy, to my mom and dad, and to my brother Noah. Finally, thank you to the Ganja: for bringing together a community of open-minded people and giving artists and thinkers an escape as good as any other. Without you, our lives would be a little less colorful.